DEADLY DISASTERS
THE JOPLIN TORNADO

BY NATHAN SOMMER

BELLWETHER MEDIA • MINNEAPOLIS, MN

Torque brims with excitement perfect for thrill-seekers of all kinds. Discover daring survival skills, explore uncharted worlds, and marvel at mighty engines and extreme sports. In *Torque* books, anything can happen. Are you ready?

This edition first published in 2022 by Bellwether Media, Inc.

No part of this publication may be reproduced in whole or in part without written permission of the publisher.
For information regarding permission, write to Bellwether Media, Inc., Attention: Permissions Department,
6012 Blue Circle Drive, Minnetonka, MN 55343.

Library of Congress Cataloging-in-Publication Data

Names: Sommer, Nathan, author.
Title: The Joplin tornado / Nathan Sommer.
Description: Minneapolis, MN : Bellwether Media, 2022. | Series: Deadly disasters | Includes bibliographical references and index. | Audience: Ages 7-12 | Audience: Grades 4-6 | Summary: "Amazing photography accompanies engaging information about the Joplin Tornado. The combination of high-interest subject matter and light text is intended for students in grades 3 through 7"– Provided by publisher.
Identifiers: LCCN 2021020928 (print) | LCCN 2021020929 (ebook) | ISBN 9781644875315 (library binding) | ISBN 9781648344398 (ebook)
Subjects: LCSH: Tornadoes–Missouri–Joplin–Juvenile literature.
Classification: LCC HV636 2011 .U6 S66 2022 (print) | LCC HV636 2011 .U6 (ebook) | DDC 363.34/9230977872–dc23
LC record available at https://lccn.loc.gov/2021020928
LC ebook record available at https://lccn.loc.gov/2021020929

Text copyright © 2022 by Bellwether Media, Inc. TORQUE and associated logos are trademarks and/or registered trademarks of Bellwether Media, Inc.

Editor: Kieran Downs   Designer: Josh Brink

Printed in the United States of America, North Mankato, MN.

TABLE OF CONTENTS

FINDING SIMBA	4
STRONG STORMS	6
DAMAGE AND DESTRUCTION	12
CLEANING UP JOPLIN	18
TORNADO SAFETY	20
GLOSSARY	22
TO LEARN MORE	23
INDEX	24

FINDING SIMBA

The Kent family hid in their basement as the Joplin tornado raged outside. But one family member was missing. Their cat, Simba, had wandered off outside before the storm!

The Kents thought Simba was lost forever. Eighteen months later, they strolled through their old neighborhood. Suddenly, Simba appeared. He ran toward them as they called his name. Together again at last!

SIMBA

STRONG STORMS

SUPERCELL

Tornadoes are spinning columns of air. They form during thunderstorms called **supercells**. Warm, **humid** air rises from the ground. It mixes with cold air. This creates strong winds. Uneven wind speeds cause the air to spin. The spinning air forms into a funnel cloud. The cloud touches the ground as a tornado!

HOW A TORNADO BEGINS

COLD AIR = ➡   WIND = ➡   WARM AIR = ➡

QUICK BUT DEADLY

Most tornadoes last less than 10 minutes once touching ground. The longest ever lasted around 3.5 hours!

The Joplin tornado struck Joplin, Missouri, on May 22, 2011. It was part of one of the largest-ever tornado **outbreaks** in the **Midwest**. The tornado touched ground near the Missouri-Kansas border. It was nearly 1 mile (1.6 kilometers) wide when it reached Joplin!

Tornado sirens sounded only 20 minutes before the storm. Many people could not prepare with such short notice.

TIMELINE

MAY 22 – 1:30 P.M.
A tornado watch is issued in Joplin

MAY 22 – 5:17 P.M.
The tornado watch becomes a tornado warning, and tornado sirens sound

TRACKING TORNADOES

Scientists use tools like weather balloons to track storms. They watch weather patterns to determine where tornadoes are most likely to happen.

MAY 22 - 5:34 P.M.
The tornado touches down southwest of Joplin

MAY 22 - 5:41 P.M.
The tornado makes its way through Joplin as an EF5 tornado

MAY 22 - 6:12 P.M.
The tornado weakens and ends southwest of Joplin

The Joplin tornado lasted 38 minutes. Winds blowing at speeds of more than 200 miles (322 kilometers) per hour struck the city. The tornado was an EF5 on the **Enhanced Fujita Scale**.

Around 50,000 people lived in Joplin when the tornado hit. Many homes and businesses were in the tornado's path.

THE ENHANCED FUJITA SCALE

EF0
wind speeds of 65 to 85 miles (105 to 137 kilometers) per hour

EF1
wind speeds of 86 to 110 miles (138 to 177 kilometers) per hour

EF2
wind speeds of 111 to 135 miles (178 to 217 kilometers) per hour

EF3
wind speeds of 136 to 165 miles (218 to 266 kilometers) per hour

EF4
wind speeds of 166 to 200 miles (267 to 322 kilometers) per hour

EF5
wind speeds of more than 200 miles (322 kilometers) per hour

DAMAGE AND DESTRUCTION

The tornado's path covered about 22 miles (35 kilometers). It hit Joplin and the surrounding area. The storm flattened entire neighborhoods. More than 7,000 homes were damaged or destroyed. This left 9,200 people without homes.

THE PATH OF THE TORNADO

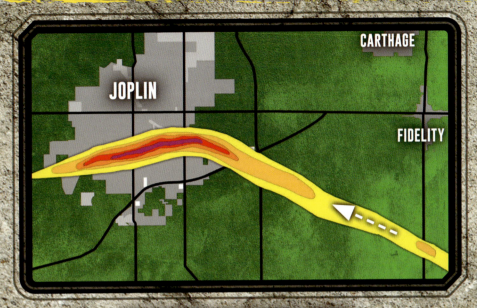

ENHANCED FUJITA SCALE RATING

EF1 = 　　EF2 = 　　EF3 =

EF4 = 　　EF5 =

The tornado sent **debris** flying. Chunks of parking lots were ripped from the ground and thrown into the air. Tools were found lodged in the walls of buildings!

The tornado ripped cell phone towers and power lines from the ground. People could not easily reach friends and family. They also could not call for help. More than 15,000 vehicles were tossed blocks away. Even semi-trucks and buses were completely destroyed. A few were wrapped around trees! Some owners never found their vehicles again.

THE TORNADO'S WRATH

After the storm, debris from Joplin was found as far as 30 miles (48 kilometers) east of the city!

The Joplin tornado injured more than 1,000 people. More than 150 people lost their lives. The tornado also caused around $3 billion in damage. It damaged 550 local businesses. More than 2,000 people lost their jobs. Some schools and offices had to be rebuilt. Returning to normal life was not easy for many people.

CLEANING UP JOPLIN

Emergency responders entered Joplin right away. They quickly set up medical centers inside tents to treat lesser wounds. Within a day, the **National Guard** arrived to help locate missing people.

Around 80,000 **volunteers** cleaned up debris after the tornado. **FEMA** supplied 586 trailers for families who lost their homes. By 2016, more than 1,600 homes had been rebuilt.

THE CIRCUS HELPS JOPLIN

The Piccadilly Circus was in Joplin when the tornado struck. Their elephants were used to help clear fallen trees and damaged cars!

VOLUNTEERS CLEANING DEBRIS

TORNADO SAFETY

Joplin is now better prepared for tornadoes. Many buildings now have **shelters**. Many homes are built to stand up to stronger winds.

More than 1,000 tornadoes strike the United States every year. People can stay safe by seeking shelter when warnings are announced. Preparation can keep people safe from tornadoes!

SHELTER

PREPARATION KIT

WHISTLE

CELL PHONE WITH CHARGER

FLASHLIGHT WITH BATTERIES

FIRST AID KIT

3-DAY SUPPLY OF FOOD AND WATER

GLOSSARY

debris—the junk or pieces left behind when something is destroyed

emergency responders—people responsible for going to the scene of an emergency as soon as it happens; police officers, firefighters, and EMTs are emergency responders.

Enhanced Fujita Scale—a way of measuring how strong a tornado is

FEMA—Federal Emergency Management Agency; FEMA gives support after all disasters that happen in the United States.

humid—having a lot of moisture in the air

Midwest—a region of 12 states in the north-central United States

National Guard—an Army branch that mostly responds to emergencies within the United States; the National Guard also helps the Army overseas when needed.

outbreaks—events in which multiple tornadoes strike the same area around the same time

shelters—places that offer protection from bad weather or danger

supercells—systems of storms that can result in tornadoes

tornado sirens—large speakers that warn people to seek safety when tornadoes are spotted

volunteers—people who complete work without being paid for it

TO LEARN MORE

AT THE LIBRARY

Levy, Janey. *Devastating Storms*. New York, N.Y.: Gareth Stevens Publishing, 2020.

Light, Charlie. *Observing Earth: Investigating Earth's Atmosphere*. New York, N.Y.: Gareth Stevens Publishing, 2021.

McGregor, Harriet. *Tornado Terror!* Minneapolis, Minn.: Bearport Publishing, 2021.

ON THE WEB

FACTSURFER

Factsurfer.com gives you a safe, fun way to find more information.

1. Go to www.factsurfer.com

2. Enter "Joplin tornado" into the search box and click 🔍.

3. Select your book cover to see a list of related content.

INDEX

businesses, 10, 16
cleanup, 18, 19
damage, 12, 13, 14, 15, 16
debris, 13, 15, 18, 19
emergency responders, 18
Enhanced Fujita Scale, 10, 11
FEMA, 18
formation, 6, 7
homes, 10, 12, 18, 20
Joplin, Missouri, 8, 10, 12, 15, 18, 19, 20
Kent family, 4, 5
National Guard, 18
neighborhoods, 12
outbreaks, 8
path, 10, 12, 13
Piccadilly Circus, 19
preparation kit, 21
schools, 16
scientists, 9
shelters, 20
Simba (cat), 4, 5
supercells, 6
timeline, 8-9
tornado sirens, 8
vehicles, 14, 19
volunteers, 18, 19
weather balloons, 9
wind, 6, 7, 10, 11, 20

The images in this book are reproduced through the courtesy of: vchal, cover (hero); Dustie, cover (debris); Wynn photography, CIP; Aaron Fuhrman/ flickr Editorial/ Getty Images, pp. 4-5; Ryan Richardson/ AP Images, p. 5 (Simba); Minerva Studio, pp. 6-7; Designua, p. 7 (tornado); tornadovideos.net/ AP Images, pp. 8-9; ZUMA Press Inc/ Alamy Stock Photo, pp. 10-11; trgrowth, p. 11; Benjamin Krain/ Stringer/ Getty Images, pp. 12-13; Globe Turner, p. 13; ZUMA/ Alamy Stock Photo, pp. 14-15; TOM UHLENBROCK/ Alamy Stock Photo, p. 15; Pierre Barlier/ Alamy Stock Photo, pp. 16-17; Sarah Conard/ Alamy Stock Photo, pp. 18-19; FEMA/ Alamy Stock Photo, pp. 20-21; Photo Melon, p. 21 (whistle); Vitali Stock, p. 21 (cell phone with charger); Petr Malyshev, p. 21 (flashlight); robertlamphoto, p. 21 (batteries); Pixel-Shot, p. 21 (first aid-kit); FabrikaSimf, p. 21 (can food); Andrey Eremin, p. 21 (water).